# The Patio Window

## A Play

Norman Stubbs

A SAMUEL FRENCH ACTING EDITION

SAMUEL FRENCH

FOUNDED 1830

SAMUELFRENCH-LONDON.CO.UK
SAMUELFRENCH.COM

# CHARACTERS

**Miss Croft**, 60s
**Nurse**, young
**Driver**, mature
**Milkman**, 25-40

The action of the play unfolds in a small Edwardian house

Time: a day in June, in the present

# PRODUCTION NOTE

Do not position the patio window in the back wall of a box set. Consider placing it in the fourth wall, as an imaginary feature (which calls for an elaborate mime from the milkman) in the form of a token structure comprising only short uprights to delineate the door frame, plus a groundrow to indicate the outer wall of the house. The advantage of this method is that most of the important lines then have to be delivered out to the front.
The only other method is to split the room diagonally: both the window and the door from the hall are then visible at forty-five degrees to the footlights.

*The Patio Window* won both the Lydia Durston Trophy, Somerset County Drama Festival 1992 and second prize : Bognor Regis Playwriting Competition 1992

---

Also by Norman Stubbs, published by Samuel French Ltd :

Ringing For You

# THE PATIO WINDOW

*The sitting room of a small Edwardian house in one of the inner suburbs of an industrial town, comfortably and tastefully furnished, but without any contemporary furniture. The main feature is a large full-length window*

*Miss Croft, an ex-teacher in her 60s, pale and unsteady in her movements, enters slowly, followed by Nurse, who is young, exuberant, very talkative, but good-hearted. Nurse looks around the room before going to look at the garden*

**Nurse** So, this is it! Number forty-seven, at last… Oh yes, and this is the famous window.

**Miss Croft** (*coming slowly down to sit looking out at the garden*) Well, I think it's very nice. Before I had it put in, you couldn't fully appreciate the garden and——

**Nurse** (*interrupting*) Yes, love, you told me. Oh yes, and what a garden. You can't see anything but greenery. (*She giggles at her own inanity*) Haven't you got any neighbours?

**Miss Croft** Of course I have. You saw as we drove up. But only on the one side; I'm the end one.

**Nurse** Lovely, yes. Still, you're in the best place; where we can look after you, and you have nice company. Yes, you're in the best place.

*Miss Croft sits wearily*

You all right, love? Sister was right: you shouldn't have come. Now then. What can I do?

**Miss Croft**  (*quite forcefully*) Nothing. Go back with the taxi driver. Where is he?

**Nurse**  Oh, poking around in the hall. (*She goes to the door*) Tom… Miss Croft wants you.

*Driver enters with a small case, which he puts down just inside the door, and a bundle of letters, which he hands to Nurse*

**Driver**  Here, you can look after these. All those leaves in the porch—soon gets neglected.

**Nurse**  They're for Miss Croft. Oh, it's mainly junk mail, I guess.

**Miss Croft**  Yes, the estate agent has picked up anything important and brought it round to the nursing home.

*Driver studies the garden through the patio window*

**Nurse**  Yes, the usual stuff: "Dear Miss Croft, you are one of six lucky persons in the Earlsdon area who have been selected…" How do they know your name? (*She goes on without a pause*) Three Peugeot two-o-five GTIs to be given away—can you drive, Miss Croft? (*She does not wait for an answer*) I think it's all a twist and——

**Miss Croft**  (*wearily*) Christine, dear, please——

**Nurse**  Luxury villas in Fuengirola, sun-kissed beaches—(*she laughs*) waste of time sending that to you! (*She is still laughing*)

*Miss Croft closes her eyes, and starts to fumble in her handbag*

Oh, this one is a bit different: it's handwritten. "To the Occupier…" Something about your window needing attention. Not signed. Don't understand it. Shall I read it to you?

**Miss Croft**  No. Christine, I really cannot he bothered with any of that now.

**Nurse** What are you looking for? Your tablets? (*She delves into Miss Croft's handbag, and produces a small pill bottle*)

*She puts one tablet in Miss Croft's palm*

Pop it under your tongue. Don't talk. Keep perfectly quiet. (*After a pause of only a few seconds*) Now what I suggest is——
**Driver** (*impatiently*) Look, you said she wanted me.
**Nurse** Oh, she said I should come back with you. But I can't, of course—can't leave her.
**Miss Croft** Christine, you can do something for me. Have a general look around the house, upstairs as well. Flush the toilets, put disinfectant down. Spiders in the bath—you know.
**Nurse** Yes, love, of course. (*She pauses at the door*) Mind what you two get up to.

*She exits, laughing*

**Driver** My God, she's got a heart of gold, I suppose, but does she get on my pip!
**Miss Croft** Yes. I'm afraid *I* find her rather exhausting. The sister said she must come with me—in case of another heart attack, but the effect she has on me increases, rather than diminishes, that possibility.

*A few moments peace. Driver looks out at the garden again*

**Driver** I'd no idea these places were so nice. I've been in one before, but...
**Miss Croft** It's the patio window, I expect. I had it put in last autumn. It seems to bring the garden right into the room. I'd miss it now if ever anything—happened.
**Driver** You'd never think you were in the suburbs—just a

stone's throw from the city centre. You could be miles away.
It's as if it's always been here—like private grounds.

**Miss Croft** Actually, it's not really a big garden, at all. I mean
it's not very long—nor very wide.

**Driver** No, but by God, it is high!

*He laughs noisily; Miss Croft does not*

Shame it's so neglected. (*He looks around the room*) Get
musty, don't they—houses—when they're left.

**Miss Croft** (*a little angrily*) It is perfectly all right. The estate
agent sees to everything.

**Driver** (*sniffing dubiously*) Does he? Where is he, anyway?
Thought he was supposed to be here to arrange about the sale.

**Miss Croft** I've no doubt that he will be here, at any moment. In
any case, I don't know that I am putting it on the market just at
the present.

**Driver** What have you come for, then?

**Miss Croft** I *had* to—had to see it again. To make up my mind
what I should do.

**Driver** Get rid of it, now. If you've got any sense. Before the
market flops again in the autumn. It's no business of mine, of
course.

**Miss Croft** (*sharply*) Indeed, it *is* no business of yours. I know
I've taken your taxi several times, and you've been very
helpful, but you must not become familiar. I do not pay you for
advice.

**Driver** No—and you don't pay me for waiting time—hanging
around. I could charge you… (*He stops short, then smiles*)
Sorry Miss, I will try to improve. Yes, my Roger told me how
you always made them toe the line—even in the sixth form. I'd
forgotten you're a teacher.

**Miss Croft** I am no longer a teacher, but I still have strong views on relationships. And there is no need for you to wait; you can come back when I've finished.

**Driver** Yes, right, (*he looks at his watch*) but I've got nothing on until the eleven forty-two Intercity gets in at the station. I'll just wait outside. (*He starts to go*) What do you want doing with the case?

**Miss Croft** Just leave it in the front bedroom.

**Driver** The front bedroom. (*He starts for the hall, then stops suddenly at the door*) You're not thinking of going up those stairs, are you?

**Miss Croft** (*impatiently*) I shall be perfectly all right.

**Driver** All right, it's no business of mine!

*She glares at him; he adopts a pose of mock humility*

Sorry! Sorry.

*He goes out to deposit the case*

*Miss Croft, with a sigh, moves to the window to look at the garden. She shakes her head*

*Driver looks in*

Right, then. I'll be out the front.

**Miss Croft** (*without looking round*) Mr Charlton.

**Driver** Yes.

**Miss Croft** Perhaps you'd care to sit down and wait in here—in comfort.

**Driver** Thank you. If I may.

*He sits, facing the window. Miss Croft potters around the room. She picks up one or two small items but looks confused by the effort. After a while, he coughs*

(*Softly*) How long has it been then?

**Miss Croft**  Oh, six months—more. Just before Christmas; I'd been trying to do some shopping. The crowds in the precinct were terrible. I don't remember it clearly, but they took me straight to the hospital—then, later on, to the nursing home. They're very good, of course, but—(*vehemently*) I hate it!

**Driver**  (*surprised at her vehemence*) But why? I should think it's quite comfortable. You're really not well, are you? Any exertion and you're done for. You're in the best place there.

**Miss Croft**  The best place! How sick I am of that phrase. Christine fusses over me until my head reels, but keeps telling me I'm in the best place. The sister implies that as soon as I step outside, I shall suffer a cardiac arrest—I know full well that it *could* happen, but I also know the statistical probability better than she does—but, nevertheless, I must remain in the *best place*.

**Driver**  Yes, I suppose you do miss your house, but——

**Miss Croft**  Miss it! (*She becomes increasingly agitated*) Miss my house? But it's not a *house*. It's far, far more than that. It's more than a home even—it's the whole purpose of my life; it's what I once dreamed of, what I slowly planned for. And when it was finally mine—the mortgage paid off—and the garden began to mature, it almost embraced me. I was content. No, that's a feeble word: I had arrived; all the wretched and painful things were in the past; it had all been worth it. Here, everything is right, and always will be—everything. But Christine and Sister and the social worker and the solicitor, they all know best: "You're in the best place". (*She is almost in tears*)

**Driver**  Yes, I know what you mean. A woman of your education, from a good class background—I know.

**Miss Croft**  Mr Charlton, how little you know. Good class! (*She assumes a strong working-class local accent*) "I'm really one of those runny nosed kids you used to see waiting on the wet pavement outside the pub".

**Driver** Good Lord!

**Miss Croft** It's been a struggle, all the way—that's why I can't be persuaded.

**Driver** But you were one of the lucky ones—clever ones. Did you get a scholarship to the Grammar?

**Miss Croft** Yes, of course, that's what everybody thinks. Wrong again. At fourteen, I was machining car seat covers in the factory—and for almost fifteen years afterwards—until I got on the teachers' training course.

**Driver** (*gently mocking*) Then you learned to speak proper, and graduated to the middle classes.

**Miss Croft** Middle classes! Oh, those classifications—far too glib. (*She looks around the room*) Yes, this is almost middle class, I suppose...

**Driver** Well, it's a bit of *luxury*, anyway.

**Miss Croft** I need very little of that. Yes, money does give you more and more things to hand around your daily routine, true. No, it's being able to choose exactly the right thing in exactly the right place. That's what really matters. I know who I am here—no one can dispute... Have you ever seen my bathroom?

**Driver** Your bathroom? Good Lord, no—how could I?

**Miss Croft** Well, it's about the same as when the house was built, I expect. But you've seen the nursing home extension, and the bathrooms there. There's *luxury*! Pampas suites, mixer taps, built-in knick-knacks—everything that money can buy, and I hate it all, hate it. No locks on the doors, no choice, no dignity. (*She becomes slightly hysterical*) I can't go on living there! (*She turns away to regain her composure*) I'm sorry to burden you with this. It's no business of yours. I'm sorry.

**Driver** (*wryly*) No, it's not *my* business. But, anyway, *I'll* not tell you you're in the best place.

**Miss Croft** But they're right, in a way, aren't they? All those who are so concerned, but don't *know*—they're sensible, of course, but they don't know it would be the death of me—not the heart disease, not that—no, leaving here. That's why I'm putting it off again. I keep pretending. Mr Ewart was almost angry.

**Driver** Ewart?

**Miss Croft** The estate agent. I've cancelled the appointment. He's not coming here. I got one of the cleaners to ring up for me. "Not yet", I said, but I don't know how much longer I can put it off. Sister would say it's to be expected—just the depression which follows a serious heart attack. I'll *have* to tell her, but please...

**Driver** (*softly*) No business of mine.

*Nurse enters*

**Nurse** What a job! I've scrubbed and scrubbed with that lav brush, but I can't shift that stain. It shouldn't have gone like that. Someone's used it and didn't pull the chain. Some man. (*She has a sudden thought*) Mr Ewart! He should know better. Wait until he gets here; I'll tell him. You shouldn't do that. I'm a nurse, and I know about these things.

**Miss Croft** (*wearily*) Christine, dear; just put some Domestos down.

**Nurse** I can't. All the disinfectant's dried up. But next time——

*Miss Croft becomes distressed. Driver signals to Nurse to keep quiet, then deliberately intervenes to silence her*

**Driver** Let's go and get some...

**Nurse** Get some what?

**Driver** From the nursing home, from my place, from Boots. Get something to clean the lav.

**Nurse** I can't. We must wait for Mr Ewart, but I'll tell him!

**Driver** (*with a wink at Miss Croft*) Oh, he's gone.

**Nurse** What do you mean—gone?

**Driver** He was only here three minutes. Come and gone.
**Nurse** Never saw him. Never heard a thing.
**Driver** Of course you didn't. Banging about with that brush, and yanking the chain.
**Nurse** Never heard a thing. So we can *all* go, then.
**Driver** Not before you've done that pan. Come on.
**Nurse** Well—but Miss Croft…?
**Driver** Will be all right. She wants to sit and rest and read her mail.
**Nurse** Sure, then, love? Shan't be five minutes. I don't like to leave it like that. Funny, at the training school, I hated to have to do the pans: now, I can't leave them alone.

*She goes out with Driver, laughing*

*Miss Croft leans back and sighs*

*Driver pokes his head back around the door*

**Driver** OK?

*She nods and almost raises a smile*

*Driver goes out*

*After a while, she takes from her handbag a list of things she has come to collect: a few small items from the desk and sideboard. Then she opens the hall door and looks up at the stairs. She puts a hand to her chest*

**Miss Croft** Oh, dear, Oh, dear.

*She goes out, leaving the door slightly ajar*

*Milkman appears outside the patio window, and attempts to*

*open it. He is twenty-five to forty, rather intense, something of a "loner". The window does not respond, so he puts down his bottle carrier, fiddles with the latch, snatches and lifts, and it opens silently. He enters the room, and from his carrier takes a jam jar of early summer flowers, which he places on the low coffee table just inside the window. He adds water from an empty milk bottle, kneeling with his back to the door*

*Miss Croft enters, unseen. Her eyes are half closed with fatigue, and she is a few paces into the room before she sees the intruder*

*For a second she is rooted to the spot. Then, with a shriek, she steps forward and swings a savage blow with her handbag, which catches Milkman across the face. He is temporarily blinded. She subsides to the floor beside an easy chair*

**Milkman** You stupid old woman. You could have blinded me. Who the hell let you in? (*He now sees that she is in distress*) Sorry, I'm only doing a few odd jobs—didn't expect anyone. Are you all right? Come on, get up. (*He helps her into the chair*) Christ, you nearly gave me a heart attack.

**Miss Croft** What are you doing here? Who said you could come in here? (*She clutches her chest*)

**Milkman** God, you look awful. Do you want a doctor? I'd better ring. (*He goes towards the phone*)

**Miss Croft** No, you can't. I had it cut off.

**Milkman** You did? It's *your* house, is it? Oh, Lord.

**Miss Croft** I'll be all right. (*She gasps for breath*) Give me my handbag.

*He hands it to her, and she takes a pill and places it under her tongue*

You'd better get out quickly, before I get the police. (*She closes her eyes, and the pain gradually subsides*)

**Milkman**  Yes, but I can't leave you like this... It's *your* house, is it? I thought no-one was... It was going to rack and ruin—such a shame. That's why I came in here—after the gales. The shed door was off its hinges...

**Miss Croft**  But who said you could? The estate agent sent you?

**Milkman**  No, no. It's just that I couldn't help noticing: as you come round the corner, this side is wide open. You could see straight in. I saw the garden—well, I've always wanted to see in. It used to be gorgeous, didn't it?

**Miss Croft**  But how could you? What about the neighbours?

**Milkman**  Well, you're the end one; when the road's empty you just walk in through the side gate. I fixed up the shed for you; it'll be all right, for a bit. Neighbours? Huh, this lot, this side, are never home during the day. And the woman down the bottom is a twit. "Can I help you?" she says. I could have been breaking in—anything.

**Miss Croft**  Who did she think you were, then?

**Milkman**  I said, "Doing a few odd jobs." Now when she sees me she waves, and says, "Back again".

**Miss Croft**  This is ridiculous. Who do you think you are? Coming into my garden, and then... Oh, you broke into the house.

**Milkman**  No, that's the whole point. I didn't break in; I'm trying to look after it. That window isn't secure—never was. Wicked, really—it's not safe. I don't know who put it in, but it was a twist: just a latch, just the basic fastener, and unless it's pushed right down, you only have to lift and snatch. Look, on an outside door like this, you should have a multi-point locking system that locks in three places, with a Yale key and—I could put you on to someone who could fit——

**Miss Croft**  Certainly not. I spent over a thousand pounds on that;

I'm not spending any more—especially now. But in any case, it's no business of yours.

**Milkman** (*after a pause*) Yes, well, I know.

**Miss Croft** I really think you must be mad. Even if I don't tell the police, I shall certainly tell your employer. Which dairy are you?

*He does not answer*

And how many times have you been in here—my living room? And the rest of the house?

**Milkman** No, never, just this room. The first time to make sure it was safe. Then I saw the garden through this window. It's lovely, isn't it—pity about that latch—and I bet it made this room, didn't it, when you had the window put in? Jeeze, you could be miles from anywhere.

*Almost involuntarily, she rises*

**Miss Croft** (*looking out beside him*) Yes, it was a bit dark in here before.

**Milkman** Now you can sit here—faces south east, doesn't it—and in the winter, when the sun is low in the sky, it comes right in and fills the room.

**Miss Croft** You've *sat* here?

**Milkman** Yes, well, once. It was blue with frost outside—just to have my sandwiches, (*sheepishly*) and on the patio, two or three times. Today, I picked the flowers—they're yours. Doing no harm. You didn't mind, did you?

**Miss Croft** Well, I don't know. I suppose...

**Milkman** Where have you been, anyway? Majorca? Tenerife? (*Defensively, getting heated*) No one seemed to care, didn't appreciate it.

**Miss Croft** (*with some irony*) Oh, I'm sorry. Am I an intruder? Do I come between you and your garden?

**Milkman**  No, no, I'm sorry. I'm being daft. It's your garden. Only, it's so marvellous; I couldn't keep away. (*He becomes lost for words. He walks over to the window and looks out*) How do you manage to get colour right through the winter? The little pinky-white blossom in January?

**Miss Croft**  Oh, that's Viburnum—Viburnum Fragans. Yes, it's never devoid of some colour. And the jasmine always seems to be in bloom.

**Milkman**  And the red one—that's Japonica, isn't it? I know that one.

**Miss Croft**  (*stepping back to look at him*) You have a nice garden?

**Milkman**  You have to be joking. I'm on the tenth floor of the Tower Block, just this side of the ring road. The Council put me there.

**Miss Croft**  So, you don't see much greenery?

**Milkman**  Funny enough, I do. Just below me is Canley Halt, where the branch line goes off. In that triangle between the lines, there's those bungalows built in the Thirties. They've all got lovely gardens—a bit overgrown, some of them. When I look down through my field glasses, I feel I'm right down there among them. I can even see into the greenhouses, sometimes. (*He laughs, a little relaxed*)

**Miss Croft**  Well, perhaps you'll have one of your own someday. (*She returns to her chair*)

**Milkman**  (*scornfully*) Yeah! Right—great, a garden of my own... When are you coming back, then?

**Miss Croft**  Ah, that's the problem. That's why I'm here. They say I mustn't come back. Just sell up.

**Milkman**  No, good God, no! You don't want to do that. You don't want to leave here! (*Self-consciously*) Not after you've spent over a thousand.

**Miss Croft**  The agent said it would add a great deal to the property, when—if—I have to sell.

**Milkman** Did he? That's all right then, I suppose. As long as you don't lose on it. But why don't you want to come back?

**Miss Croft** Oh, I'd love to; it may not be possible, that's all. When they took me away, I thought I could come home, one day after I'd had the bypass.

**Milkman** You had the what?

**Miss Croft** Bypass—heart surgery—you know. It's quite commonplace nowadays.

**Milkman** So, why not?

**Miss Croft** Well, the tests showed it had gone too far. "Occluded arteries" they call it—sounds liked geology, doesn't it? Not much chance of any improvement—not at my age, anyway.

**Milkman** You could manage, though—with help.

**Miss Croft** Possibly I could—for a while, perhaps.

**Milkman** So now you're trying to decide?

**Miss Croft** Yes.

**Milkman** Nice if you could—for the summer... The wallflowers want sorting out, don't they?

**Miss Croft** They've gone all woody. They want throwing out, then start again.

**Milkman** Start again. Yeah, that's it—start again. (*After a long pause. Softly*) And I do odd jobs, you know. Start at half four, finish midday. I've nothing else. Plenty of time in the afternoon—you know—for odd jobs.

**Miss Croft** What, like hanging shed doors?

**Milkman** Yes, that's it—shed doors (*he laughs tentatively*) and general security.

*For a few seconds they laugh together quite relaxed*

I used to call here once. Perhaps you'd like me to call again.

**Miss Croft** (*pulling herself together*) Well, thank you, but I don't think I'll have any need for... I expect you keep pretty busy, anyway.

**Milkman**  What, spying on the back gardens in Canley Close? (*With renewed eagerness*) Of course, we do eggs and butter, and cream and cheese. I can get potatoes, in fifteen pound bags. And Christmas, we have——

**Miss Croft**  Steady on, it's only June. Christmas is a long way off.

**Milkman**  But you never know, do you? Shop early for Christmas! You never know.

**Miss Croft**  (*with a strange gravity*) No, indeed, you never know... (*She pulls herself together*) But nothing at all today, thank you, milkman.

**Milkman**  Yes, well... Oh, I did leave a note through the letter box. Just throw it away.

**Miss Croft**  Thank you, I shall look. I shall find it. Thank you.

**Milkman**  Yes, well. Just leave an empty bottle out if you want me to call. (*He looks at his watch*) Jeeze, he'll crucify me. (*He goes towards the window, and looks out at the garden, then purposefully takes an empty milk bottle and places it on the coffee table*) You may need that. I'll leave it, just in case.

*Without looking at Miss Croft, he goes out swiftly, closing the window behind him*

*Miss Croft sits looking at the garden, until she remembers the note, which she retrieves from the pile. She returns to her seat, and reads it*

*Driver enters*

*She folds the note, puts it in her handbag, and only then looks up*

**Driver**  You don't really want to be bothered with this, do you? I managed to leave her behind, but the sister is very angry, and says I must bring you straight back. So let's be having you... You all right? You look pretty rotten. Do you want to sit for a bit?

**Miss Croft**  I'm all right, don't fuss. There's just the case.
**Driver**  Where is it?
**Miss Croft**  Where you left it.
**Driver**  Why? Haven't you got your things?
**Miss Croft**  I couldn't be bothered.
**Driver**  Bothered! You couldn't manage the stairs, could you?
  I'm beginning to think they're right. Perhaps you are in the best
  place.
**Miss Croft**  (*vehemently*) Please mind your own business. I can
  come again. I can get my things next time.
**Driver**  Will there be a next time, Miss Croft? Are you coming
  back—honestly?
**Miss Croft**  (*very sharply*) I shall be in the car.

*She goes straight past him into the hall*

**Driver**  (*starting to follow her, but turns at the door and sees the
  milk bottle*) Let's leave the place a bit tidy.

*He picks up the bottle and goes out*

*After a few seconds, raised voices are heard off stage*

**Miss Croft**  (*off*) What have you got there?
**Driver**  (*off*) It's only an old milk bottle.
**Miss Croft**  (*off*) Leave it alone. I want it left—left there.

*She enters, a handkerchief covering her mouth. She is carrying
the bottle*

I may need it. (*After a moment's reflection she comes slowly
but purposefully down and places it on the coffee table. She
bends to tidy up the flowers, but seems at first afraid to look*

*directly out. Then she looks up and scans every corner of the garden. She straightens up, and steps slowly back towards the door. Softly)* The best place?

*Soft plaintive music—such as the* Adagietto *from Mahler's* Fifth Symphony—*accompanies her as she looks off, takes two deep breaths, and goes out slowly, closing the door behind her*

*The music increases in volume for a little, and then the Lights fade, leaving only a soft pool on the table and the bottle. The music and the Lights fade as——*

*—the* CURTAINS *slowly close*

# FURNITURE AND PROPERTY LIST

Further dressing may be added at the director's discretion

*On stage:*    Desk
Sideboard
Low coffee table
Phone

*Off stage:*    Small case, letters and note (**Driver**)
Handbag. *In it:* small bottle of pills, list (**Miss Croft**)
Bottle carrier. *In it:* jam jar with early summer flowers,
milk bottles—one filled with water (**Milkman**)

*Personal:*    **Miss Croft:** handkerchief

# LIGHTING PLOT

Property fittings required: nil
Interior. The same throughout

*To open:* Overall general lighting

| | | |
|---|---|---|
| *Cue* 1 | The music increases in volume<br>*Fade lights, except a soft spotlight on the table* | (Page 17) |
| *Cue* 2 | The music fades<br>*Fade spotlight* | (Page 17) |

# EFFECTS PLOT

<table>
<tr><td>Cue 1</td><td>Miss Croft: "The best place?"<br>Music: Adagietto from Mahler's Fifth Symphony</td><td>(Page 17)</td></tr>
<tr><td>Cue 2</td><td>Miss Croft exits<br>Increase volume a little; fade out when ready</td><td>(Page 17)</td></tr>
</table>

# Last Scene Of All

## A play

Margaret Wood

*Samuel French – London*
*New York – Sydney – Toronto – Hollywood*

# CHARACTERS

**Dame Anthea**
**Francesca**
**Bobbie**
**Cherry**
**Gladys**
**Antony Redfern**
**Arthur Pendragon**

The action of the play takes place in the lounge of the
Gwynne-Garrick Home for Retired Artistes

Time: the present

# ABOUT THE CHARACTERS

**Dame Anthea**—an ample, impressive, Shakespearian actress of the Grand Manner.

**Francesca**—a lean, intellectual Ibsenite actress.

**Bobbie**—an *ingénue passée*. Her accent is the pinched, refined speech of the 1930s.

**Cherry**—a showgirl who, having no occasion to speak on stage, has had no need to improve her accent, which betrays her origins as different from those of the others. She has, however, kept her figure.

**Gladys**—Anthea's dresser. She is the realist who does her job thoroughly and observes life keenly and intelligently, though her origins are the same as Cherry's.

**Antony Redfern**—a dapper, lively, little man.

**Arthur Pendragon**—a classical actor from the same school as Dame Anthea.

All the characters are, alas, definitely Senior Citizens—though no one admits it, except Gladys, who doesn't think about herself much.

# LAST SCENE OF ALL

*The lounge of the Gwynne-Garrick Home for Retired Artistes*

*The lounge is comfortably furnished (a curtain set is the most suitable background) with these essential pieces of furniture: a screen UR across the corner; a small drinks table UL; an armchair RC with a settee angled L beside it; a small table in front of the settee; DR a writing table with a chair or stool in front of it and DL an ironing board and iron with stools or chairs either side for piles of ironed and un-ironed clothes. Other chairs, flowers etc can be added to dress the stage if space permits*

*As the* CURTAIN *rises Francesca is seated at the writing desk, in profile, writing a letter. Anthea is in the armchair leafing through a large book of press cuttings. Bobbie is on the settee, putting out playing cards on the small table in front of her whilst beside her Cherry is buffing her nails. Gladys stands at the ironing board, ironing steadily*

*There is an opening silence, during which Gladys finishes one garment, lays it aside and takes up another. Then Anthea sighs heavily*

**Anthea** All, all are gone, the old familiar faces . . .

**Francesca** Whose old familiar faces?

**Anthea** "These precious friends, hid in death's dateless night."

**Bobbie** Oh, Anthea! You're looking at your old press cuttings again. You shouldn't you know, you really shouldn't. It always depresses you.

**Anthea** (*placing her hand lovingly on a photograph*) Timothy Jordan, for instance. Such a lovely witty Mercutio he was. (*In a conversational tone*) Actually, I preferred him to my Romeo in that production. So slim, dear Timothy, an eagle's talon in the waist.

**Gladys** Didn't stay that way, did he?

**Anthea** (*sighing*) No. He ended up playing Falstaff without padding. Lord, lord, "we know what we are, but know not what we may be".

**Gladys** (*automatically*) *Hamlet*, Act Four, Scene Five.
**Francesca** (*without looking up*) That's right. Ophelia running mad in white satin.
**Anthea** (*turning on her*) Ophelia does *not* run mad in white satin! She runs mad in whatever she happens to be wearing at the time.
**Francesca** My dear Anthea I was quoting from—
**Bobbie** (*excitedly*) Oh, look. There's a stranger in the cards. Tall dark and handsome.
**Cherry** (*looking*) Ooh! Anyone we know?
**Gladys** Wouldn't be a stranger if we did, would it?
**Cherry** The Warden did say there was a new resident coming. A gentleman.
**Anthea** What sort of gentleman?
**Cherry** There's only one sort of gentleman. Otherwise he isn't one.
**Anthea** I mean is he straight, classical, comic or music hall?
**Bobbie** The cards don't tell you things like that. That's their agent's job.
**Anthea** (*reflectively*) Tall, dark and handsome ...
**Francesca** (*impatiently*) Oh Anthea. This stranger is just a playing card plus Bobbie's fertile imagination. I'm trying to write a letter.
**Anthea** There's the writing room.
**Francesca** Yes, and it's full of old men dozing behind their papers or reminiscing about their glorious careers.
**Gladys** Whereas this room is full of old women doing the same thing.
**Francesca** Or seeing tall dark strangers in the cards.
**Bobbie** (*re-dealing the cards*) It's sad, you know. It really is. You don't believe in what the cards foretell, do you?
**Francesca** No, I don't. The future is quite bleak enough without meeting it halfway.
**Bobbie** Let me tell you, Francesca, I've seen things in these cards. Things that would surprise you.
**Francesca** I'm not easily surprised.

*Pause. Anthea closes her book, sighs, rises restlessly and puts the book on the drinks table, moves upstage and drapes herself against the backcloth,* c

**Anthea** "Aye me. My little body is aweary of this great world!"
**Gladys** Stands to reason. It's been in it a long time.

**Anthea** (*turning majestically*) What has?

**Gladys** Your little body. Not so little now, either.

**Anthea** There's no need to be personal, Gladys. I was merely quoting from Shakespeare.

**Gladys** (*impatiently*) I know that! M.O.V., Act One, Scene Four.

**Cherry** M.O.V.? What's that?

**Gladys** *The Merchant of Venice.*

**Cherry** (*losing interest*) Oh. . . . Shakespeare . . .

**Bobbie** I thought it was something like V.A.T.—

**Cherry** Or M.O.T.

**Francesca** You would, Bobbie. A career beginning with *Bunty Pulls the Strings* and ending with the twenty-fifth year of *The Mousetrap* is hardly conducive to culture.

**Bobbie** (*indignantly*) What do you mean? I bet I've as much culture as you have. I've had a lot more variety in my work than either of you.

**Anthea** (*coming downstage*) "Variety" being the keyword.

**Francesca** The Tiller Girls wasn't it, Cherry? Or the Windmill?

**Anthea** (*loftily*) I never could distinguish between the Tiller Girls and the Windmill Girls. Both sound so very wooden.

**Cherry** (*rising indignantly*) There was nothing wooden about the Windmill Girls! And we never closed. All through the bombing and the black-out, we never closed.

**Francesca** (*folding her letter and putting it in an envelope*) You never moved, either.

**Cherry** (*plaintively*) We weren't *allowed* to move, were we? The Lord Chamberlain said we could be nude as long as we didn't move. That was the law.

**Francesca** Naked tableaux for tired business men in the front rows, goggling through opera glasses.

**Cherry** At least the front rows were full. That's more than could be said for some of your high class joints.

**Bobbie** *And* you never closed. Most companies shut up shop and took culture to the provinces.

**Cherry** Mind you, I sometimes thought it would be better if we *had* closed during the winter. I could stand the bombs, but not the goose pimples. (*She walks round the back of the settee to* c, *lighting a cigarette as she goes*) I shall never forget the night when a bomb fell next door and poor old Lord Mortchester died in the middle of Row B.

**Bobbie** Goodness! Did it hit him?

**Cherry** No. I *told* you. It fell next door. They *said* it was shock. (*She shrugs*) Well, I suppose it was, in a way.

**Anthea** What do you mean, "in a way"?

**Cherry** Sort of indirectly. He was sweet on Babs Bouncer at the time, you see. Lovely statistics that girl had. Well, when the bomb dropped, *she* jumped, see? Well, we all did. But Babs jumped more than most. (*Sighing*) The excitement killed the poor old boy.

**Gladys** Lovely way to go, though.

**Anthea** (*emotionally*) "How oft, when men are at the point
                              of death
                    Have they been merry!" ...

**Gladys** (*automatically*) R and J, Act Five, Scene Three.

**Bobbie** R and J?

**Gladys** *Romeo and Juliet.* In the tomb.

**Bobbie** A tomb? How morbid. I've never acted in a *tomb*. I was offered a part in a coffin once. *Dracula* it was. But I turned it down. "Nothing morbid", I said. "A murder or a bit of adultery if you like, but it's got to be good clean fun."

**Francesca** (*sarcastically*) Such as *Rookery Nook*, I suppose.

**Bobbie** (*unaware*) That's right. I *loved* being in *Rookery Nook*.

**Cherry** Gladys, how come you know all this Shakespeare stuff— M.O.V. and R and J and that?

**Gladys** Because I've been Dame Anthea's dresser for over thirty years. While I was dressing her we used to go through her parts, didn't we, madam?

**Anthea** Not that I *needed* the words, you understand, but it got me in the mood.

**Gladys** Oh yes, I knew all her parts *and* the bits before and after.

**Anthea** The cues, dear, the cues.

**Gladys** That's right. Mind you, I've never known the plays all through. Just chunks where she had something to say.

**Anthea** Really, Gladys, you speak of Shakespeare as if he were a tin of pineapples.

**Gladys** I never saw any of the plays right through either; I wonder sometimes what happened. That Romeo, for instance.

**Anthea** What about him?

**Gladys** All that palaver and poison in the tomb. He made a right bloomer over that, didn't he?

**Francesca** How?

**Gladys** When he shinned down that rope off the balcony, why didn't he take her with him? After all, they *were* properly married. It would have saved a lot of trouble all round.

**Francesca** But there wouldn't have been a play, would there, Anthea? You're quite right, Gladys. (*She takes a book and begins reading*)

**Anthea** Ridiculous!

**Gladys** (*to Anthea*) And you *could* have shinned down a rope with the best of them in those days.

**Anthea** You don't shin *down* a rope, Gladys. Only up . . . True. I could have done either. I was an athletic little thing.

*Bobbie and Cherry giggle—Anthea glares at them*

And I could *still* play in *Romeo and Juliet*—as the Nurse. I've always wanted to, but it never came my way

*Anthea advances towards Francesca. She breaks into ribald laughter and slaps Francesca on the back with a vigour that sends her book flying*

"And then my husband—God be with his soul!
A' was a merry man—took up the child:
'Yea,' quoth he, 'dost thou fall upon thy face?
Thou wilt fall backward when thou hast more wit;
Wilt thou not, Jule?"

**Francesca** (*irritably retrieving her book*) Oh, for heaven's sake—!

**Anthea** (*turning and poking Bobbie*)

"I warrant if I should live a thousand years
I never should forget it. 'Wilt thou not, Jule?'
   quoth he.
And pretty fool, it stinted and said 'Ay'."

**Francesca** (*shouting her down*) Oh do shut *up*, Anthea. The Nurse is supposed to be a garrulous old bore, but that's no reason why you should bore *us*.

*Anthea flounces away upstage. There is a pause*

**Cherry** (*to Bobbie*) Very *noisy*, Shakespeare, isn't it? The Windmill was ever so quiet. Refined, by comparison.

**Anthea** (*turning on Francesca*) Of all the prize bores, Francesca DARLING, Ibsen is the worst and Shaw runs him a close second. I remember seeing you as Hilda Wangel in *The Master Builder*. (*She pauses significantly*)

**Francesca** And what about me as Hilda Wangel in *The Master Builder*?

**Anthea** (*acting it*) Standing there, facing left, into the wings, because that's your better side, and waving to a non-existent old man on a non-existent tower and crying—"I hear a song on the air. Do you hear harps? Look, look! He's waving his hat. Wave back to him, wave, wave, The Master Builder! MY Master Builder." (*Turning: flatly*) No wonder the old fool fell off.

**Francesca** (*springing to her feet and facing her: a tiger*) I'd have you know that the critics said I made that tower so real to them that they experienced a feeling of vertigo.

**Anthea** So did I. For a different reason. (*She floats around waving and mocking*) "Do you hear harps in the air?" Gladys, do you hear harps?

**Gladys** Not yet. Any time now.

**Francesca** You're a cat, Dame Anthea. A cat with a very limited range. You don't understand Ibsen. You don't understand symbolism.

**Anthea** Symbolism, dear, is a thing the critics invent when they don't know what on earth the play's about. It's like doctors telling you you've got a virus. It means they don't know.

**Francesca** Such ignorance is beyond belief. And you are a Dame! A pantomime dame would be more appropriate.

*Antony Redfern enters upstage* R, *smoothly passes between the two contestants during the following speech and exits downstage on the opposite side*

**Anthea**            "You were a vixen when you went to school
                       And though you be but . . ."
(*In the same breath*) . . . who *is* that dreadful little man?

**Gladys** He's a resident. You've seen him about.

**Cherry** But what's the *matter* with him? He's always drifting in and out—

**Bobbie** He never speaks to anyone except at meals. Just walks by as if he didn't see you.

**Gladys** That's where you're wrong. He thinks you can't see *him*.

He once took the name part in Wells' *Invisible Man*. Never got over it.

**Francesca** (*crossing and helping herself to a drink from the table*) Really this place gets crazier every day. And we shall go crazy too if we don't stop fratching over the past, Anthea. Have a drink. (*She hands her one*)

**Anthea** (*gracious*) That's very sensible of you, dear. We must guard against petty-mindedness. Girls! Have a snifter. It's nearly dinner time.

*Bobbie and Cherry go up for drinks: Gladys continues to iron: Anthea sits down on the settee*

**Francesca** The trouble is, we lack something positive to *do*.
**Gladys** Like ironing.
**Francesca** Gladys, get yourself a drink and have a rest.
**Gladys** Thanks. I will. (*She goes to the table and returns to sit in the chair* L)

*Cherry perches gracefully on the left end of the settee. Bobbie sits in Francesca's former chair* DR

**Bobbie** There. Now we're all cosy let's think of something positive.
**Cherry** How do you do it? Is it a game?
**Anthea** Not exactly, dear. It's an exchange of ideas.
**Francesca** Ideas! About how to keep busy and active and avoid scratching each other's eyes out.
**Cherry** (*looking blank — then brightening*) I can crochet a bit.
**Anthea** I was thinking of a communal effort. After all, we *are* trained in team work. So . . . ?
**Francesca** We ought to be thinking about our Christmas entertainment. The men did it last year, so it's our turn. Surely we can do better than their effort.
**Bobbie** (*giggling*) They *were* a bit crummy, weren't they? All those wobbly baritones and quavery tenors pretending to be pirates or policemen.
**Cherry** (*giggling*) And those rickety tap dancers with white tie and tails and walking sticks that got between their legs.
**Anthea** Now! I have an idea. Why not do a very dignified, very beautiful, imaginatively lit and marvellously spoken Nativity play?

*Pause*

**Francesca** Not very original.
**Anthea** (*snappy*) Neither is Christmas.
**Gladys** You mean US?
**Anthea** (*vaguely*) And a few others. We can scrape up a Joseph and the odd shepherd.
**Bobbie** They'll be *very* odd.
**Gladys** What about the Virgin?

*Pause*

Well, come on. None of us qualifies.
**Anthea** What about that little maid that waits at table?
**Gladys** I said virgin. That maid's no maid. (*She returns to her ironing board*)
**Francesca** I agree. I'm not particularly religious, but there is a limit. That girl's beyond it.
**Anthea** (*impatiently*) All right, ALL RIGHT! No virgins available. Nativity play's out. Religion's out. Somebody else suggest something.
**Bobbie** What about *A Christmas Carol*? Nice and topical.
**Francesca** And how many women's parts would you have in that? It's nearly all men. Can you see the Invisible Man as Tiny Tim?
**Cherry** What about a pantomime?
**Gladys** Plenty of Ugly Sisters.
**Bobbie** We'd need a handsome Prince.
**Cherry** (*giggling*) The gardener's a bit of all right.
**Bobbie** And a Buttons. We must have a Buttons.
**Cherry** Oh, do you remember little Tony Redfern as Buttons? Wasn't he a marvellous acrobat? He could pop up through trap doors and disappear through walls—

*Antony Redfern enters* L, *crossing in front of the settee*

**Bobbie** And so versatile. He could play anything, from Shakespeare to *Charley's Aunt*. (*Sighing*) Oh, Tony Redfern!
**Redfern** (*pausing; to Bobbie*) You called?
**Bobbie** (*startled*) Pardon?
**Redfern** Antony Redfern.
**Bobbie** Yes. I was talking about him.

*Gladys continues ironing*

**Redfern** Now you see him. Antony Redfern in person. How do you do?

*Bobbie makes a cooing noise of pleasure. He goes round all of them till he comes to Gladys*

How do you—*Gladys!*
**Gladys** (*quietly*) Hallo, Tony.
**Redfern** Where did you spring from?
**Gladys** My springing days are over. I've been ironing in this corner for the last two years.
**Redfern** I've never noticed you before.
**Gladys** (*drily*) No. I was invisible.
**Redfern** Now then Gladys, now then. You always were a cheeky girl. (*Turning to the others*) Actually I have ceased to be invisible because of a change in circumstances. "And what is that?", I hear you ask . . . Do I hear you ask?
**All** And what is that?
**Redfern** I have a friend coming to live here! A dear old friend. Legit. and classical actor. He will be a great asset to our happy band. Excuse me, if I vanish for the present.

*Redfern goes* UR, *watched by the others, and "disappears" behind the screen*

**Cherry** (*disappointed*) He seems to vanish like anyone else. I thought he'd go all shivery and melt away.
**Anthea**          "O! that this too too solid flesh would melt,
                   Thaw, and resolve itself into a dew . . ."
**Gladys** *Hamlet*, Act One, Scene Two.
**Anthea** (*sharply*) How do you know that bit? I'm not *on* when he says that.
**Gladys** Oh, I heard other people's lines besides yours, you know. Hamlet's included.
**Anthea** Hamlet's? Arthur Pendragon's lines? *You* heard them for him? You never told me.
**Gladys** No, you wouldn't have liked it then.
**Anthea** I don't like it now. *When* did you hear his lines? You were *my* dresser.
**Gladys** When I wasn't running after you, I helped *him*. Only in the wings, so you needn't worry.
**Anthea** I don't believe a word of it.

**Gladys** (*shrugging*) Please yourself.
**Anthea** And I do object to you ironing my things in the public lounge. Can't you do them in your room!
**Gladys** No plug. It's a second class room.
**Anthea** God give me patience!

*Anthea sweeps out*

**Francesca** I don't know how you stand it, Gladys. There you are, working all day to make her comfortable and she has to find something to complain of.
**Gladys** (*tolerantly*) It's a habit.
**Bobbie** Well, get out of it. You're retired and independent now.
**Cherry** She'd be lost without you.
**Gladys** I'd be lost without her.
**Francesca** Well, you shouldn't let her ride roughshod over you.
**Gladys** I'm tough. Besides, she's forgotten all about it the minute after. You'll see. She'll be back here all smiles in no time.
**Bobbie** You know what I think? She's jealous of you hearing Arthur Pendragon his lines. He's *her* property.
**Gladys** He *was*. They haven't met for years—not since he told her she was past playing the Portias and Violas and Mirandas and had to go on to the heavies.
**Francesca** Glory! That must have been a drama.
**Gladys** It was. They were doing *The Tempest* at the time and he'd found a new youngster to play Miranda. The only thing left for Anthea was a harpy. So she quit. He went to Stratford, Ontario; never came back. Married that little Miranda—for a time.
**Cherry** He was a lovely looking feller though. Could have fallen for him myself.
**Gladys** Most women did. Especially Anthea.

*Anthea enters, brandishing a small green book*

**Anthea** (*triumphantly*) I've got it, dears, I've got *just* the thing for our Christmas entertainment. *The Trojan Women*!

*Pause*

**Francesca** (*incredulously*) For *Christmas*?
**Anthea** Why not. A great play for a great Festival.
**Francesca** But Christmas is a festival of birth and hope: *The Trojan Women* celebrates death and destruction.

**Cherry** What did they do, these Trojan Women?

**Francesca** Howled, most of the time. Very loudly.

**Anthea** Of course I knew *you'd* be down on it, Francesca, because you hadn't thought of it. But I'll be generous. (*Graciously*) You can be Antigone.

**Francesca** I'd rather be Cassandra.

**Anthea** Oh, very well. Type-casting, of course, but perhaps that's safer.

**Francesca** Which version are we doing?

**Anthea** Gilbert Murray's, of *course*.

**Francesca** Why of course? The National's done a new prose version. I thought it was marvellous.

**Anthea** There, if I may say so, you show your lack of literary appreciation. Gilbert Murray wrote poetry. The National's version is in the language of waiters!

**Bobbie** Some waiters have very nice language. French sometimes: or Italian. According to the menu.

**Anthea** WE ARE DOING THE GILBERT MURRAY VER-SION!!

**Francesca** Have it your own way. (*Mischievously*) Who are playing the gods?

*Anthea checks a little and looks uncertainly at the cast list in her copy*

**Bobbie** Oh, I've never been a god. Can I be a god, please? Please!

**Anthea** (*looking up: with finality*) The gods are cut.

**Gladys** You'd forgotten the gods, hadn't you?

**Anthea** (*turning on her*) No gods are available. We shall be hard put to it to find enough ordinary mortals.

**Cherry** What can I play?

**Francesca** Helen of Troy, I should think. She was a dumb blonde too.

**Anthea** Yes, dear. Helen.

**Cherry** I can just stand still, can I? (*She poses*)

**Francesca** No. You have a long speech. Very long.

**Cherry** Oh dear. I'm not used to that. I don't think I can learn a long—

**Anthea** Bobbie will be Andromache.

**Francesca** Oh, Anthea, do be *sensible*. Andromache has a heart-rending scene with the child. You can't expect Bobbie to—

**Bobbie** (*furiously*) And why not? What makes you think I can't rend hearts? I can rend them all right, if I have to. I've never been given the chance, that's all.

**Anthea** I, of course, shall be Hecuba.

**Francesca** Of course.

**Anthea** And so we have a play fitted! What a brainwave! I've always wanted to do *The Trojan Women*. Now, the staging is going to be difficult—

**Gladys** Especially as we haven't got a stage.

**Anthea** We'll have to use the dining room again, I suppose. It's the biggest.

**Francesca** (*gloomily*) It's only got one door.

**Anthea** That screen. We could put one screen across a corner, and another somewhere else and make two more entrances.

**Bobbie** Bit amateurish, isn't it?

**Anthea** Now dear. That's a word we don't use here. We are professionals. Amateurs are those dreadful people who enter through the fireplace, wear wrist watches in *Julius Caesar* and forget to take off the Virgin Mary's wedding ring. Bobbie, Cherry, bring that screen across here will you?

*Cherry and Bobbie obey, one each end of the screen, sliding it along the floor. Behind it, unseen, moves Redfern. He stops in a dramatic pose centre, while the screen moves on, suddenly revealing him. Cherry, having placed the screen, turns and almost bumps into him*

**Cherry** Oh my gawd. He *can* make himself invisible—he can!

**Francesca** Don't be a fool, Cherry. It's one of the oldest tricks in the business. (*Severely*) You've been listening, haven't you, Mr Redfern?

**Redfern** Indeed, yes. Most interesting. May I ask—?

**Anthea** Be quiet, little man. I must work this out ...

**Francesca** Anthea, you can't be serious. We haven't enough people. There's a *Chorus* of fifteen to start with.

**Anthea** The Chorus is cut.

**Gladys** Look, dearie. You've cut the gods: you can't cut the Chorus too.

**Redfern** And what about the men?

**Anthea** The what?

**Redfern** The men. It occurs to me, for example, that there is a Messenger. There has to be. There always is.

**Bobbie** Why?

**Redfern** Because, dear lady, in Greek plays, nothing ever happens *on* the stage.

**Cherry** (*interested*) Oh! Just like the Windmill Theatre. I shall feel at home with that.

**Redfern** So there has to be a Messenger who rushes in and tells everybody about it. Like this. (*He goes* UR *and then rushes* DC)

"Oh, woe, woe, woe! Unutterable woe!"

(He then proceeds to utter unutterable woe. As follows)

"Your son, my lord, is torn apart by horses.

(*To Anthea*) Your husband, queen, has sacrificed your daughter

To get a following wind. For which foul deed His queen (that's you) has felled him with an axe

(*To Cherry*) But tidily, in his bath, to save the mess. A good domestic touch. Your son, in turn

Despatches you as well. ...

And then there's a bit of incest here and there to give variety. For instance:

(*To Francesca*) Your son, in error, married with his mother Who hanged herself in consequence. And he, Full of remorse, put out his eyes ...

—off stage, of course, but he comes in looking extremely bloody and unpleasant.

(*Generously*) I'll be the messenger, dear lady. There's more in it than I thought.

**Anthea** Well ... I ...

**Cherry** You *can* cut my speech, can't you? If I could just stand. (*She poses*)

**Anthea** No.

**Cherry** Well, p'raps you could write it out and pin it to the back of a sofa or chair or something ...

**Anthea** No chairs, no sofas.

**Cherry** Oh, Anthea. I do like a nice set with a three piece suite and French windows and a fireplace with a glow and ...

**Anthea** It's not that sort of play!

**Redfern** And another little matter. What about Menelaus?

**Anthea** (*apprehensively*) What about Menelaus?

**Redfern** He has an important scene with his adulterous wife Helen.

**Cherry** Here! Nobody told me I was adulterous.

**Anthea** Couldn't we cut Menelaus?

**Francesca** No, we could NOT! For heaven's sake, he and his wife are the *cause* of the whole Trojan War. He's frightfully important.

**Anthea** (*throwing the book on the settee*) The title is most deceptive. I thought it was an all-women play! Why, *why* call it *The Trojan Women* when it's full of tiresome men?

**Redfern** If I might make a suggestion?

**Anthea** Another?

**Redfern** Yes. My friend who arrives in time for dinner.

**Bobbie** My stranger—in the cards! Is he tall, dark and handsome?

**Redfern** That would describe Sir Arthur Pendragon in his prime, I suppose.

**Gladys** *WHO* did you say?

**Redfern** Sir Arthur Pendragon. You must have heard of him.

**Anthea** Arthur? Arthur Pendragon? (*She sinks, swooning picturesquely, on the settee*) The wheel has come full circle. My heart bursts smilingly.

**Francesca** He's coming *here*?

**Redfern** Indeed yes. He approaches, he is nigh. The train arrived fifteen minutes ago.

**Cherry** Isn't it a lovely name? Arthur Pendragon. So romantic.

**Gladys** (*drily*) When I first knew him he was Percy Phipps. Snotty-nosed little boy. Lived in the same street as us. In Neasden. But he improved.

**Anthea** Arthur—the ideal Menelaus! His dignity, his curling hair upon his brow, his thrilling voice ... Oh. This will bring back the heyday in the blood. "The nobleness of life is to do thus"! Don't tell him I'm here (*Fluttering*) Let it be a surprise.

*Redfern exits*

How shall I greet him? Where shall I stand?

**Francesca** (*mischievously*) Well, he'll come in there (*She points* L). Suppose you go down there and turn only *after* he's come in. Then you'll see the joyful recognition in his eyes.

**Gladys** (*to Francesca*) That's cruel. One of your real Hedda Gabler bits, that is.

*Anthea goes* DL, *practising turning and greeting*

**Anthea** What shall I say? (*Turning, arms outstretched*) Arthur, my
own!
**Bobbie** "Arthur, my own?" Sounds like the plays I used to be in.
**Francesca** It *is* a bit P. G. Wodehouse.
**Gladys** You actors make me sick. Why can't you just say,
"Arthur, how lovely to see you", and give him a big hug?
You've spent all your lives spouting other people's words and
haven't any of your own left. Second-hand, the lot of them.

*Gladys snaps the ironing board together and goes out with it,
angrily*

**Anthea** (*still downstage practising*) I've a better idea. I'll greet him
with something we've done together. Something that will take us
back thirty ... well, something that will take us back. How
about this. ... ?
(*Simply*)        "You see me, Lord Bassanio, where I stand,
                    Such as I am. (*Turning upstage*) Though for myself
                        alone
                    I would not be ambitious in my wish
                    To wish myself much better. ..."
**Francesca** They're coming! Off everyone, off! Leave them
together.

*Francesca herds them all behind the screen*

*Gladys comes in and begins to collect her ironing*

*Arthur Pendragon enters. He is about seventy, balding, stooping,
with a stick. Redfern follows with the luggage*

*Anthea takes up her pose. Pendragon surveys the scene sourly*

**Anthea**        "You see me Lord Bassanio where I stand,
                    Such as I am ... (*She turns and sees him*)
                        Though for ...

(*She turns away, stunned by what she has seen*) Oh, what a fall
was there!
**Pendragon** (*to Redfern; irritably*) I knew it was a mistake. I should
never have listened to you, Redfern. How do you expect me to
live here with such dreary nonentities? Some old frump there (*he*

*points with his stick*) reciting the Merchant. You needn't bring that luggage any further. Put it back in the taxi.

**Redfern** (*beaming*) Taxi's gone.

**Pendragon** Then phone for another.

*Redfern goes, shrugging*

**Anthea** Oh, sharper than a serpent's tooth . . . (*She sinks weeping on to the settee*)

*Gladys comes behind Pendragon, a pile of ironing in her arms*

**Gladys** Percy Phipps!

*Pendragon starts and turns*

If you're going to be personal, just you remember the lean and slippered pantaloon. That's *you*. So don't be patronising, because I won't have it.

**Pendragon** Gladys! It's my dear old Gladys. Well, well! *You* haven't changed anyway.

**Gladys** (*composedly*) No. My mother always used to say "You've never looked young or pretty, Gladys, but you'll look no worse when you're older". Very comforting, that's been. Nothing to lose. Not like some.

**Anthea** (*speaking into a cushion*) I can't bear it, I can't bear it.

**Gladys** (*pointing to Anthea*) Just look what you've done. *That* is Anthea.

**Pendragon** That? My God! She's gone off a bit.

**Gladys** So have you.

**Pendragon** You mean to say she was that old bird spouting the Merchant when I came in?

**Gladys** She was greeting *YOU*! A special performance. And you never noticed.

**Pendragon** Oh God, what a brute I am! (*He strikes a repentant pose*)

**Gladys** Put it right. Now. Cheer her up.

**Pendragon** How can I? It isn't possible to get round a gaffe like that.

**Gladys** Try Shakespeare.

**Pendragon** "Try Shakespeare", she says. She offers me the whole of the Shakespeare canon and expects me to select, at a moment's notice!

**Gladys** King Lear. Act Four, Scene Seven. Recognition scene. And do it well. You didn't always. And I'm not staying to prompt. You're on your own.

*Gladys exits*

**Pendragon** (*taking a deep breath*) Recognition scene ... Ah yes. Just the job.

*Pendragon ages visibly, turns and totters slowly to sofa. The actor playing Pendragon should do this as well as he can, without guying it: they are, after all, supposed to have been fine actors. He sits dejectedly and uncertainly beside Anthea, looks at her, then speaks to audience*

> "Pray, do not mock me
> I am a very foolish, fond old man,
> Fourscore and upward, not an hour more or less,
> And to deal plainly,
> I fear I am not in my perfect mind ..."

*Anthea raises her head and looks at him tremulously: he returns her gaze*

> "Do not laugh at me:
> For as I am a man, I think this lady
> To be my child Cordelia."

**Anthea**           "And so I am, I am!"

**Pendragon**        "Be these tears wet? Yes, faith. I pray, weep not."

**Anthea** (*suddenly recovering*) Oh, I'm not really. (*She blows her nose*) I was humiliated rather than hurt, so don't apologize. I ought to have more sense. Gladys is right. We don't live real lives, we actors. We just can't face the fact that we're finished. Oh, that reminds me. Will you play Menelaus in *The Trojan Women*?

**Pendragon** That self-righteous old cuckold? Certainly not. (*Pause. He is tempted*) When are you doing it?

**Anthea** (*happily*) For Christmas.

**Pendragon** *The Trojan Women*? Ye gods, what a choice. No, sorry.

*Anthea begins to protest*

I can't. I am probably going back to Stratford, Ontario for my final FINAL performance ... Or perhaps my semi-final.

**Anthea** Oh, Arthur. So soon. We meet but to part?

**Pendragon** (*suddenly inspired*) Tell you what. Why not come with me, Anthea? You and I—the famous old partnership together again. It would be tremendous box office. We could do scenes— full lengths are beyond us now. Scenes for the . . . er . . . the more *mature* actor—like Henry Eight and Katherine, Leontes and Paulina, Lear and Goneril—you could still do Goneril at a pinch . . .

**Anthea** (*rising; ecstatic*) Mistress Page and Falstaff—Oh, Arthur, what a heavenly idea! I'll come, of course I'll come.

*Gladys enters*

Gladys, we're going to Stratford, Ontario—and touring afterwards. You too, of course. You'll have to go through my hamper and make sure we've got the costumes.

**Gladys** (*resigned*) We have. They're always ready. I know what to expect.

**Anthea** Good, good. Won't Mr Redfern be thrilled?

*Anthea and Pendragon exit* L

*Gladys sighs, sits on the settee and takes out a cigarette. Cherry and Bobbie and Francesca come out from behind the screen*

**Cherry** Did you hear that? A tour in Canada! Do you think they'd take me?

**Gladys** No.

**Bobbie** Or me? I'd do anything—a maid or housekeeper—anything.

**Gladys** Not a chance.

**Francesca** You seem remarkably calm, Gladys. I thought all you wanted was to put your feet up and stay put.

**Gladys** That's right. And that's what I'm doing.

**Cherry** Well, you won't be able to do it on tour.

**Gladys** (*scornfully*) Tour? There'll be no tour. By dinner-time they'll either have quarrelled over the programme or forgotten that they ever suggested it.

**Cherry** But they sounded so serious.

**Bobbie** And excited.

**Gladys** Acting, dear, acting. Just remembering what they used to be like. They'll soon be excited by something else. You'll see.

*Anthea sweeps in,* DL

**Anthea** Darlings! Such a surprise! Sir Arthur—

*Pendragon and Redfern enter*

—has decided to stay here with us— with ME!

*All burst into applause. Pendragon bows, kisses Anthea's hand and she drops a deep curtsey*

**Pendragon** Madam you have bereft me of all words.
**Gladys** Like to bet on it?
**Anthea** Just think, dears. We have our Menelaus! We can do *The Trojan Women* after all.
**Pendragon** Good God! No, Anthea, not that, not that! I'll go to Ontario rather than play Menelaus.
**All** Hear, hear!
**Anthea** Oh well, we'll think of something else.
**Redfern** (*climbing onto a chair*) Friends, Romans and all the rest of you, I have an idea!
**Francesca** Not another!
**Redfern** *I* will produce a pageant suited to the talents of all present.

*During Redfern's allocation of parts the company busily seize something to give them a feeling of the character; Anthea winding her pearls in her hair as a crown, Francesca throwing a black scarf around her, Bobbie seizing flowers from a vase, Pendragon a cloth from the table, Cherry a toasting fork and a round tray as a shield etc*

You, Cherry shall be Britannia.
**Cherry** (*hopefully*) No moves, no speeches?
**Redfern** None. It's a posing part. Bobbie shall be a flower girl singing her sweet lavender in old London town.
**Bobbie** Oh, Audrey Hepburn in *My Fair Lady*!
**Redfern** Francesca shall be—er—Mary Queen of Scots and Anthea, Queen Elizabeth . . .
**Pendragon** And I?
**Redfern** Either the Earl of Essex or Sir Walter Raleigh. Both have good death scenes.
**Gladys** What about me?

**Anthea** Oh, you'll be doing the costumes, dear.
**Gladys** Thought so.

*Gladys exits*

**Redfern** (*shouting*) Now, pose! Get in the mood!

*Cherry strikes a provocative pose as Britannia, Bobbie wanders around warbling "Buy my sweet lavender", Francesca kneels tragically by a chair and bows her head with outstretched arms, Anthea cries "Off with her head," while Pendragon casts the table cloth at her feet. They build to a noisy pyramidical tableau with Britannia at the apex, standing on the settee, while Redfern shouts*

That's the idea. Hold it, hold it. Head a bit higher, Anthea; head a bit lower, Francesca; voice a bit softer Bobbie; face a bit more this way, Arthur . . .

*Gladys enters with her ironing board and a stage costume and proceeds to iron as*

the CURTAIN *falls*

# FURNITURE AND PROPERTY LIST

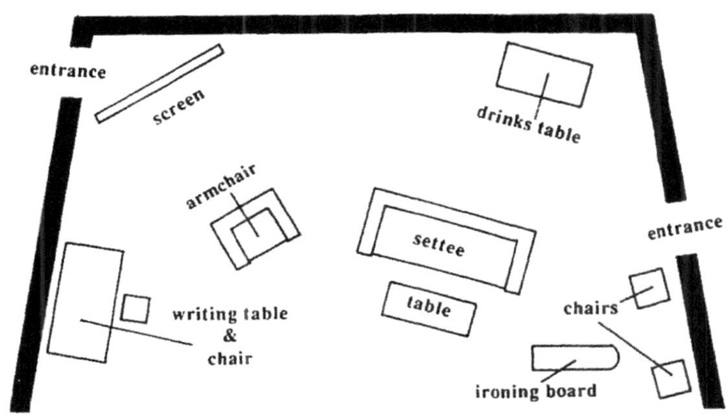


*On stage*:   Screen
Drinks table. *On it:* glasses, bottles
Armchair
Settee. *On it:* cushions
Small table in front of settee. *On it:* cloth, playing cards
Writing table. *On it:* pen, paper, envelopes, books
Chair at writing table
Ironing board. *On it:* iron
Two chairs with piles of ironed and unironed clothes
Vase of flowers
Black scarf
Toasting fork
Round tray
} Set where appropriate

*Offstage*:   Small green book (**Anthea**)
Luggage (**Redfern**)

*Personal*:      **Anthea:** press cutting book, pearls
                 **Cherry:** manicure set, cigarettes and lighter
                 **Pendragon:** stick
                 **Gladys:** cigarettes and lighter

# LIGHTING PLOT

One interior setting. No fittings required.

No cues

www.ingramcontent.com/pod-product-compliance
Ingram Content Group UK Ltd.
Pitfield, Milton Keynes, MK11 3LW, UK
UKHW021819150726
7214IPUK00017B/207